The Bungle Gang Strikes Again

David Walke

Hutchinson

London Sydney Auckland Johannesburg

To Sophie, Aidan and David

Hutchinson Education
An imprint of Century Hutchinson Ltd
62-65 Chandos Place
London WC2N 4NW

Century Hutchinson Australia Pty Ltd
89-91 Albion Street, Surry Hills,
New South Wales 2010, Australia

Century Hutchinson New Zealand Limited
PO Box 40-086, Glenfield, Auckland 10,
New Zealand

Century Hutchinson South Africa (Pty) Ltd
PO Box 337, Bergvlei 2012, South Africa

First published 1985
Reprinted 1987, 1989

Set in Linotron 202 Rockwell by
Wyvern Typesetting Limited, Bristol
Printed and bound in Great Britain

British Library Cataloguing in Publication Data

Walke, David
    The Bungle Gang strikes again. – (Spirals)
    1. Readers – 1950-
    I. Title
    428.6'2   PE1121
ISBN 0 09 162571 8

Contents

The Secret Stamp Testers

6 parts: Boss, Billy, Flash, Post Office Lady, PC 22, Sergeant

Scene   Outside a Post Office

Boss	You can't park the car here, Billy.
Billy	Why not?
Boss	It's on my foot! YEEOW!
Billy	Hang on, Boss. Don't go away. I'll back the car up.
Boss	How can I go away?! YEEOW! I've got a car on my foot!
Billy	Is that OK, Boss? Is it off your foot?
Boss	Yes, now get out of the car and bring the masks. Where is Flash?
Flash	I'm here, Boss. Is that the Post Office?
Boss	Yes, that's the Post Office. Let's get the masks on and do the job.
Flash	Where are the masks, Billy?
Billy	Here they are.

Boss	Oh, no! These are no good!
Billy	These were the only masks I could get. I got a rabbit, a duck, and a mouse.
Boss	I'll be the mouse.
Flash	Give me the duck.
Billy	I want the duck!
Flash	You can't have the duck, Billy. Here's the rabbit. Put it on.
Boss	Shut up, you two! Put your masks on! We have to move fast.
Billy	Look, this mask has only got one hole for my eyes.
Flash	You've got it on upside down, fool! You're looking out of the rabbit's mouth.
Billy	Oops, I am a silly Billy. I'll turn it round.
Boss	Come on, we have to move fast. Let's get over to the Post Office!
Flash	OK, Boss.
Billy	It's locked.
Boss	What?
Billy	The door is locked.
Boss	It can't be locked! Push it hard!
Billy	It's locked. It's shut. I can't get it open.

Boss	Kick it!
Billy	OK ... YEEOW! My foot!
Boss	There's a window in the door. Can you see inside?
Flash	Yes, here comes an old woman.
PO Lady	What do you want?
Boss	We want to come in.
PO Lady	You can't! I'm having my cup of tea.
Flash	You've got to let us in.
PO Lady	Why?
Billy	We've come to rob you.
PO Lady	What?!!
Boss	No! No! Don't listen to him. We just want some stamps.
Billy	Yes, we've come to nick your stamps.
PO Lady	What? You've come to nick my stamps?!
Boss	No! No! We've come to LICK your stamps. He said LICK, not NICK!
Flash	Shut up, Billy. Keep your trap shut, or we'll never get in!
PO Lady	Why do you want to lick my stamps?

Flash	We're from London. We're from the GPO. We have to test your stamps.
PO Lady	Why?
Boss	To see if they stick, you silly old bat!
Flash	They keep falling off the letters. So we have to test them.
Boss	So will you let us in?
PO Lady	It sounds a bit funny to me. Why have you got masks on?
Flash	We're under cover.
Boss	We're secret stamp testers. We have masks on so that you won't spot us.
PO Lady	Rubbish! I can spot you a mile away with masks like that. You look funny!
Flash	Yes, that's right. We want to be funny secret stamp testers.
Boss	We like being funny. We like to make people happy. It's for Christmas.
PO Lady	Where is your card?
Billy	It's parked over there.
PO Lady	I said CARD, not CAR.
Boss	What card?

PO Lady	If you're from the GPO then you'll have a card.
Billy	But it's not my birthday.
Flash	She means your pass card, Billy.
Billy	My bus pass?
Flash	That's a good idea, Billy. Show her your bus pass. That will do the trick.
Boss	The rabbit has got the pass. Open the door and he'll show it to you.
PO Lady	OK, I'll open it. Give me the pass.
Flash	Open the door a bit more. We can come in and show you the pass.
PO Lady	No, I've got the chain on the door. Just hand the pass to me.
Billy	Here it is.
Boss	Push your way inside, Billy!
Billy	I can't – she's got the chain on the door.
Flash	Well, stick your foot in the door. Try to stop her shutting it.
PO Lady	This isn't a GPO pass. It's a bus pass. I'm going to shut this door and lock it!

[*Bang*]

Billy	Yeeow! My leg!
Boss	Oh, no! Here's a copper!
Flash	Run for it! Get into the car!
Boss	Come on, Billy.
Billy	Hey, Boss, come back.
Flash	Come on, Billy!
Billy	I can't! I've got my trousers stuck in the door. The old woman jammed them when she slammed the door!
Flash	Oh, no! Boss, come back. Billy is stuck. The old woman jammed his trousers in the door.
Boss	Oh, no. It's a pity she didn't jam his head as well!
Billy	What shall I do?
Boss	Cut his trousers. Get a knife. Cut him loose!
Flash	I haven't got a knife.
Boss	Then Billy will have to take his trousers off.
Billy	I will NOT!
Flash	Oh, yes you will. Get them off, and then we can get away.

Boss	Hurry up. That copper has seen us!
Billy	I will NOT take my trousers off in the street.
Flash	Then I'll do it for you.
Billy	No! YEEOW! Get off!
Flash	I'll hold the trousers, Boss. You get hold of Billy, and pull him out.
Boss	OK, I'll get hold of his head and pull.
Billy	No! No! Get off! Get off!
PC 22	Hello, hello, hello. What's going on here?
Boss	Nothing, officer.
PC 22	Then can you tell me why the duck is trying to pull the rabbit's trousers off?
Boss	Well ... emmm ... it's like this ....
PC 22	And can you tell me why YOU are trying to pull the rabbit's head off?
Boss	Well ... emmm ... he's not a real rabbit!
PC 22	I see.
Flash	And I'm not a real duck.
PC 22	I can tell that by your feet.
Billy	They were trying to pull my trousers off.
PC 22	I can see that.

11

Billy	I got them jammed in the door.
PC 22	I don't like this. I don't like it at all. I'm going to call my sergeant on my radio.
Flash	Now we're in for it.
Boss	I love it when a plan comes together.
PC 22	This is PC 22. Come in, Sergeant. Can you hear me?
Sergeant	This is the sergeant. What do you want?
PC 22	I've got something.
Sergeant	Go home and go to bed. Take some tablets. That will make it go away.
PC 22	This is PC 22 calling the sergeant. It's not a cold, sir. I've got three of them here. They want to get into the Post Office.
Sergeant	You've got three of them? What are you talking about? Three postmen? Three turnips? Three hamsters?
PC 22	No, Sergeant, there's a mouse, a duck, and a rabbit ....
Sergeant	Are you OK, 22? Have you been at the wine gums again?
PC 22	No, sir. There are three of them here. The mouse and the duck were trying to pull the rabbit's head off ....

Billy	They were trying to get my trousers off!
PC 22	The rabbit says they were trying to get his trousers off ....
Sergeant	So the rabbit has got trousers on?
PC 22	Not any more, sir. I need help here.
Sergeant	I think you need help too. I think you need a doctor!
PC 22	Can you send a van round?
Sergeant	I just did. It's on its way.
Flash	We'll never get out of this.
Boss	I wish you would keep your mouth shut, Billy.
Billy	What's the matter? I just said we were robbing the Post Office, that's all.
PC 22	Aha! So you were going to rob the Post Office!
Boss	Oh no, Officer, don't listen to him. He doesn't know what he's saying. He's had a bang on the head.
PC 22	When did he have a bang on the head?
Boss	Soon!
Sergeant	Are you still there, 22?
PC 22	Yes, Sergeant.

Sergeant	Are the rabbit and the mouse and the duck there too?
PC 22	Yes, Sergeant. The rabbit's had a bang on the head.
Sergeant	I think you have as well!
Boss	This is a big mistake, Officer. We aren't really trying to rob the Post Office.
PC 22	It is a big mistake, and you're the one who made it!
Sergeant	Are you still there, 22? The van is on its way.
PC 22	I'm still here, Sergeant. You'd better hurry up. The mouse is trying to talk his way out of it.
Sergeant	Well, give him a piece of cheese, and tell him to keep his trap shut.
Flash	Can't you give us a break?
PC 22	Yes, a jail break. Now then, let's have those masks off. I want to see who you are.
Boss	I'm Boss, this is Billy, and this is Flash.
PC 22	Pleased to meet you. Here's a white van coming now. This must be it.
Boss	It doesn't look like a police van.
Flash	It looks like an ambulance.

Billy	It's stopping.
PC 22	Hello, Sergeant. There's a white van here. But it's not the police van.
Sergeant	That's right, 22, and can you see the two men in white coats?
PC 22	Yes, Sergeant, they've got hold of my arms.
Sergeant	That's right, 22. They've come to take you away for a little rest. It's just till you stop seeing mice and ducks and rabbits robbing the Post Office.
PC 22	But wait! Get your hands off me! It's true! It's true! They were trying to rob the Post Office!
Sergeant	That's right, 22. Just go with the nice men. You can have a long rest.
Billy	What's going on, Boss?
Boss	Well, Billy, I think we just got let off the hook!
Flash	What do we do now?
Boss	Run, Flash! Just run!
PC 22	Come back! Get off me! They're getting away! Help! Police!!
Sergeant	Bye bye, 22, bye bye ....

15

The Mouse Trap

4 parts: Boss, Billy, Ma Boss, Flash

Scene Boss's house

[*KNOCK! KNOCK!*]

Boss	Who is it?
Billy	It's me. Let me in. [*Steps inside*] Where's the money, Boss?
Boss	Look, tell me who you are! Who? WHO!?
Billy	I can hear an owl. Have you got an owl in your house, Boss?
Boss	Oh, it's Billy! Come on in. Stop messing about. I'm in the kitchen.
Billy	Hello, Boss. Have you got an owl in your house?
Boss	No, but I think you've got bats in your head!
Billy	Where's the money, Boss?
Boss	It's on the table. We'll split it up when Flash gets here.

Billy	Wow! We've never nicked so much before. Look at it all, Boss!
Boss	Not now, Billy. I'm looking for something for a mouse.
Billy	What about cheese?
Boss	I mean poison, Billy.
Billy	I don't think the mouse will like poison.
Boss	Look, you twit, I want to get rid of the mouse!
Billy	Oh no, Boss! Why do you want to get rid of a sweet little mouse?
Boss	It's been in the fridge.
Billy	That's not fair. I've been in your fridge too, but you don't try to get rid of me.
Boss	That's a good idea!
Billy	I've got an idea, too. Just let the owl loose. The owl will get rid of the mouse.
Boss	I think I'll get an eagle. That will get rid of both of you!
Billy	Shall I count the money out, Boss?
Boss	No, Billy. Keep your hands off it. We'll split the money when Flash gets here. Get me a cup of tea.

Billy	OK, Boss.
Boss	I've found the mouse-hole. It's here in the wall. It goes into the cupboard under the stairs.
Billy	I think I'll have a cup of tea, too.
Boss	This mouse must have teeth like a shark!
Billy	How's that?
Boss	This hole goes right into the wall.
Billy	You'll have to go in after it, Boss.
Boss	You're right, Billy. You'll have to go in after it! Do you know how to catch a mouse?
Billy	No, Boss, but I know how to catch a rabbit.
Boss	How?
Billy	Hide behind a bush and make a noise like a carrot.
Boss	Look out, Billy. You're spilling tea all over the money.
Billy	Sorry, Boss.
Boss	Now, come here and help me. Look, the mouse-hole goes into the cupboard under the stairs. You go into the cupboard and

	make a big noise. The mouse will run out here and I'll get it.
Billy	OK, Boss, I'll get in. Ooh! It's dark in here!
Boss	Shut the door and keep still. Can you see the hole?
Billy	Yes, I'll get down beside it. I can't see the mouse yet.

[*KNOCK! KNOCK!*]

Boss	Don't make the noise till I tell you. Just a minute, there's someone at the door. It must be Flash.
Ma	Hurry up, son. Open the door.
Boss	Oh, no! It's not Flash. It's my Ma!
Billy	What's the matter, Boss?
Boss	Quick, Billy, come out! It's my Ma! Help me! Hide the money! Don't let her find out that I've been nicking stuff again! She'll kill me!
Billy	Where shall I hide it, Boss?
Boss	I don't know! I don't care! Stick it up your jumper! Hurry up!
Billy	OK, Boss. Will this do?

Boss	Oh, no! That's no good. Don't let Ma see you like that! Get back in the cupboard! You look like a turnip!
Ma	Hello, son, are you in there? What's going on?
Boss	Don't say anything about the money, Billy. We'll pretend we are still looking for the mouse. I'll get rid of Ma as fast as I can. Shut the door.

[*KNOCK-KNOCK-KNOCK*]

Boss	It's OK, Ma. I'm coming.
Ma	Hello, son, where have you been? I've got you some fish and chips for your dinner.
Boss	Thanks, Ma, I'm starving. Give them to me. Look at the time, Ma, it's time for you to go.
Ma	Don't be silly! I've just got here! What are you doing, son?
Boss	I'm trying to catch a mouse. That's the hole, down there.
Ma	Yes, I can see it. I'm going to have a look at it.
Boss	Ma, I don't think this fish is cooked. It just ate one of my chips.

Ma	It's a big mouse-hole.
Boss	I'm going into the kitchen to get some salt for my chips.
Ma	Hello, mouse, are you in there?
Billy	Hello? Yes, I'm still here.
Ma	AAGH! It spoke! The mouse spoke!
Billy	It's me. It's Billy.
Ma	Good grief, it's got a name! The mouse is called Billy! Ooh, I think I'm going to faint! Ooh, help! Ooh, ooh, oooh!!
Billy	Boss, I can hear the owl again.
Boss	Aagh! Here it is! The mouse is in the kitchen! Don't let it get away! Don't let it get in the hole! Get back, mouse! Get back! Back! Back! Back!
Billy	I can hear a duck now, Boss. But I still can't see the mouse.
Ma	There are two of them! The mouse in the hole is shouting at the mouse in the kitchen!
Boss	Look out, Ma, it's running for the hole! Catch it!
Ma	Oh no, I can't, I can't! Horrible little mouse!

Boss	Go on, Ma, move! Catch it! Move! Move! Move!
Billy	You're not going to believe this, Boss, but I can hear a cow now.
Ma	Aagh, no!
Boss	Oh, too late! It's gone in the hole.
Ma	I need to sit down. Oh, what a shock I got.
Boss	Hang on, maybe Billy got it. Billy, did you see the mouse?
Billy	Yes, Boss.
Boss	Did you get it?
Billy	No, Boss.
Boss	Why not?
Billy	It just ran up my leg! Aagh, get off! Help! Help!
Ma	Oh, my goodness, what's all that noise?
Boss	It's that mouse!
Ma	This is too much for me. I'll have to go and lie down soon.
Boss	Oh, good!

[*KNOCK-KNOCK*]

Boss	There's a knock at the door. Who is it this time?
Flash	It's me. Hello, Boss. Hello, Ma.
Boss	Come in, Flash. Don't talk about it.
Flash	Don't talk about what?
Boss	Don't talk about the money.
Ma	What's that? Did you say money?
Flash	Shhh, Ma! Boss says we haven't got to talk about it.
Ma	Have you been up to your tricks again? You told me you had stopped. If you've been robbing banks I'll bop you with my hand-bag!!
Boss	My goodness, it's getting late. What time is your bus, Ma?
Billy	Aagh! Help! Get it off me! Aagh!
Flash	What's all the noise?
Boss	I've got a mouse.
Flash	A mouse? It's making a lot of noise. It must be six feet tall with army boots on!
Ma	What!? The mouse is six feet tall! I'm going to faint. Call me a doctor!
Flash	OK, you're a doctor.

Boss	Call her an ambulance. Maybe it will take her home. Billy is in the cupboard with the mouse, Ma. It's Billy that is making all the noise. I'll show you. Come out here, Billy.
Billy	OK, Boss. Hello, Ma.
Ma	Hello, Billy. You've got very fat all of a sudden. He looks like a turnip. Why has he got pound notes sticking out of his jumper?
Boss	Oh, no! It's nothing, Ma .... Get back into the cupboard, Billy. Get that money out of your jumper!
Billy	OK, Boss.
Ma	Have you been robbing banks again?
Boss	Not me, Ma. I haven't been near a bank for weeks!
Billy	Here I am. I'm thin again.
Boss	Look, let's forget about the money. What about the mouse? I have to catch that mouse.
Flash	Why do you have to catch the mouse, Boss? What harm can it do? What has it done to you?
Boss	Look! Somebody's been eating my bread.

And somebody's been eating my cheese.
And somebody's been eating my cake,
and they've eaten it all up!

Billy   Who do you think it was, Boss?

Flash   It sounds like Goldilocks to me.

Boss   It wasn't Goldilocks, it was that mouse! I
          know you're in that hole, mouse. I'll
          catch you!

Flash   You need a cat, Boss.

Ma   He hasn't got a cat.

Boss   The lady next door has got a cat.

Billy   I'll go and get it.

Flash   Send the cat into the cupboard. A mouse
          is no match for a cat.

Billy   Here's the cat.

Boss   Give it to me. In you go, cat. Get the
          mouse!

          [BANG-CRASH-SQUEAK-BANG-MEE-OUCH
          ... KNOCK-KNOCK-KNOCK-KNOCK]

Billy   That sounds like the cat banging on the
          door.

Flash   It wants to come out. I'll open the door.

Ma   Oh, no! Look at that poor cat!

Boss	My goodness! It's got a black eye and a cut lip!
Flash	It's got lumps of fur missing. What's been going on in there?
Billy	You would think that a cat could get one little mouse!
Flash	We'll have to try something bigger. What about a dog?
Ma	Where will we get a dog?
Boss	The lady next door has got a dog.
Billy	I'll take the cat back and get the dog.
Boss	We'll get it this time. One little mouse will be no match for a dog!
Flash	I hope the dog knows that.
Billy	Here's the dog. Open the cupboard door.
Boss	In you go, dog. Get the mouse!

[BANG-CRASH-SQUEAK-BOW-OUCH-CRASH-BANG KNOCK-KNOCK-KNOCK-KNOCK]

Flash	Oh, no! Now the dog is banging on the door! Let it out!
Billy	My goodness, what a mess!

Ma	The poor dog is all scratched!
Flash	How can one mouse do that to a dog?
Boss	Hand me that torch. I'm going to have a look in that cupboard.
Flash	It sounds like you've got Super-mouse in there, Boss!
Boss	Stand back. I'm going in.
Billy	It made a real mess of the cat and the dog.
Boss	No wonder! There's not just one mouse, there are two of them! This means war!
Flash	He's flipped his lid. We are never going to get the money split up at this rate.
Boss	There's only one thing for it. Get the old goat!
Billy	Come on, Ma. Boss wants you.
Ma	What a cheek! I'm not an old goat!
Boss	I don't mean my Ma, you fool. The lady next door has got an old goat.
Billy	OK, Boss, I'll go and get it.
Boss	I'm sick of this. Now I've got two mice. I'll send the goat into the cupboard. They'll not know what has hit them!

Billy	Come on, you smelly old goat! Help me, Flash. I'll pull his rope. You get round the back and push.
Flash	No, Billy. I'll pull the rope. You can go round to the back and push.
Ma	This is too much for me. You're all mad!
Boss	Get it into the cupboard.
Billy	It's in! Shut the door!
Boss	Now you're for it, you horrible little mice!
	[*CRASH-BANG-SQUEAK-BANG-CRASH*]
Ma	I'm going home. This is a mad-house. Goodbye!
Flash	Hooray, she's gone. Can we split the money now, Boss?
	[*BONG-CRASH-BONG-CRASH*]
Boss	You'll have to wait. We can't get the money until the goat has finished.
Flash	Why?
Boss	Billy hid the money when Ma came. It's in the cupboard with the mice and the goat.
	[*MUNCH-MUNCH-MUNCH-MUNCH* ...]

Flash	It's gone quiet in there, Boss. What's that noise?
Billy	I think the goat is eating something.
Flash	I hope it's not the poor mice.
Boss	That old goat eats anything. It eats grass and flowers and carrots. It even eats paper!
Billy	It eats paper!?
Flash	Boss! The money!
Boss	Yes, that old goat is daft enough to eat money! But who would give it pound notes to eat?
Flash	Where's the money, Boss!?
Boss	It's in the cupboard ... AAAAAAAGH!!!!

[*MUNCH-MUNCH-MUNCH*]

Christmas Crackers

4 parts: Boss, Billy and Flash (together inside a reindeer outfit), The Snowman

Scene A foggy Christmas Eve in a dim, dark street.

Billy	Why are you dressed as Santa Claus, Boss?
Boss	It's the best way to get into a house at Christmas.
Billy	Why are we dressed as a reindeer, Boss?
Boss	I'm Santa Claus, so I've got to have a reindeer.
Flash	We feel a bit daft dressed as a reindeer. Can we take this outfit off?
Boss	But what if somebody sees me? What if they ask me where my reindeer is?
Flash	Just wish them a Happy Christmas, and tell them you had to come on the bus because it's foggy.

Boss	Don't be stupid. Santa doesn't come on a bus!
Billy	It's all right for Flash. He's at the front end with the reindeer's head. How come I'm at the back end?
Boss	Flash is at the front end because he's got a big red nose.
Billy	It's not much fun at the back end.
Flash	Well, it's not much fun being at the front either. I've got these big antlers on my head. They are very heavy.
Boss	I wish you two would shut up. It's hard trying to find a house to get into with all this fog. I keep getting lost.
Flash	I wish you would.
Boss	I don't know where we are. I think that house over there has got an upstairs window open.
Flash	Yes, Boss, it's hard to see in the fog, but I think the window is open.
Boss	OK, Billy, I'll let you out. I'll pull the zip. The reindeer outfit comes apart. Now you can stand up.
Billy	The reindeer's back legs fit me like trousers.

Flash	I feel a fool standing here with this reindeer's head on. Can I take it off, Boss?
Boss	No, don't take it off. If somebody comes I'll have to zip you both back together fast. Now, let's get into that house!
Billy	How are we going to get up to that window, Boss. Have we got a ladder?
Boss	No, I couldn't get it in my sack.
Flash	How are we going to do it, Boss?
Boss	Can you see that old shed at the back of the house?
Flash	Yes, Boss.
Boss	I'll stand on Billy's shoulders. I'll get on to that shed at the back of the house. Then I'll get up the drain-pipe to the window.
Flash	What do you want me to do?
Boss	Stand on the corner and watch for coppers. We'll get into the house. Then we'll open the front door and let you in.
Flash	OK, Boss. I'll keep watch.
Boss	Don't let anyone see you.
Flash	Don't be stupid, Boss. I've got a

reindeer's head on. EVERYBODY will see me!

Boss	OK, we'd better hurry up. Come here, Billy. Let me stand on your shoulders. Here I go.
Billy	Can you make it, Boss?
Boss	No, I can't reach to get on to the shed.
Billy	Well, let me stand on *your* shoulders, Boss. I'm taller than you. Maybe I can reach.
Boss	OK, let me come down. Now then, get on to my shoulders. That's it. Can you reach?
Billy	No, I can't make it. Can you jump up and down?
Boss	Not with you on my shoulders, you fool. Come down and we'll start again.
Billy	Look, Boss, here are some old wooden boxes. Let's put them next to the shed.
Boss	That's a good idea! Flash, come and shift these boxes!
Flash	OK, Boss.
Boss	Now, help me up on to the shed. Come up with me, Billy.

Billy	OK, Boss, I'm up. What do we do now?
Boss	I'm going across the top of the shed to the drain-pipe. Then I'll go up the pipe to the window.
Billy	OK, Boss, but watch it. This shed seems a bit old.
Boss	Don't worry, Billy, I know what I'm doing.

[*CRRAAASHH!!!!*]

Flash	What's all that noise?
Billy	It's the Boss. He's gone.
Flash	Where has he gone?
Billy	Through the roof of the shed.
Flash	I thought he was going up the drain-pipe.
Billy	So did he.
Boss	Flash! Can you hear me?
Flash	Yes, Boss, where are you?
Boss	I'm in this rotten old shed. Help me to get the door open.
Flash	Are you OK, Boss? Did you get hurt when you fell?
Boss	No, I didn't get hurt. I landed on my head.

Billy	Are you coming up again, Boss?
Boss	Just a minute, Billy, I'm not Spider-Man! Help me on to these boxes, Flash, and watch what you're doing with your antlers!
Flash	There you are, Boss. Up you go.
Boss	Now, where is that drain-pipe?
Billy	It's over there, Boss. Look out for the hole in the roof.
Boss	OK, I'm going up the drain-pipe. Then I'll be able to get in the window.
Billy	Yes, Boss, but look out, that drain-pipe looks old and rusty.
Boss	Oh, shut up, Billy. I've been going up drain-pipes for years. You can't tell me about drain-pipes. AAAGH!!
	[*CRRAAASHHH!!!!!*]
Flash	What's the matter now?
Billy	It's the Boss.
Flash	What's he done this time?
Billy	The drain-pipe snapped off. He's gone through the roof of the shed again.
Flash	How are you going to get into the

	window now, Boss? The drain-pipe has snapped.
Boss	I'm going to fly up there, fool! You will have to come up on to the shed with us. You and Billy can lift me up to the window.
Flash	Come on, then, let's get on with it.
Boss	Now, Billy, I want you and Flash to help me up to the window. Get hold of a leg each and lift me up.
Flash	Don't drop him, Billy, or you'll split him up the middle!
Boss	That's fine, I'm up to the window, and it's open. I'm trying to get in. Give me a little push. Not too hard! AAAAGHHH!!
	[*BUMP-BUMP-BUMP-BUMP-BUMP-CRASH!!!*]
Flash	Oh, no! Where has he gone now?
Billy	Help me up, Flash, and I'll have a look.
Flash	Can you see anything?
Billy	Yes, this window is at the top of some stairs. We pushed Boss in and he went right down the stairs.
Flash	He went in with both feet this time.
Billy	He's got a terrible bump on his head.

Flash	That must be his nose.
Billy	No, this is too big for his nose.
Flash	Help me up, Billy, I want to see.
Billy	Come on up. Now, look down there. Look at that bump. What a mess!
Flash	That's not a bump, Billy. It's a big white flower-pot. Boss has got his head stuck in a flower-pot. He must have landed in the pot when he fell down the stairs! Let's go down and help him.
Billy	It's OK, Boss, we're here. Let's get this thing off your head.
Boss	Oh, my head! Let me feel it. Oh, my goodness! My head has gone all hard! All of my hair has dropped out!
Flash	No it hasn't, Boss. That's not your head you can feel, it's a pot. You've got your head stuck in a pot.
Billy	I'll try and pull it off, Boss.
Boss	Ooh! Ouch! Get off, Billy!
Billy	What are we going to do, Flash? Why don't I smash the pot with a hammer?
Boss	Because you'll smash my head as well, fool!
Billy	What are we going to do?

37

Boss	Look, I can't stay here in a Santa Claus outfit with a pot on my head. I look like a bottle of tomato sauce. Somebody might come back. Grab what you can, then we'll get back to my house.
Flash	OK, Boss, you stay here. Billy and I will have a look around.
Boss	Hurry up. Fill my sack.
Billy	Wow! There's a big Christmas tree in here!
Flash	Put it down, Billy. We're not taking that.
Billy	Here's a big turkey, Boss. Shall I put it in the sack?
Boss	Is it dead?
Billy	I hope so. I've just had a bite out of its leg.
Boss	Put it back, Billy. We don't need a turkey. I've got one at home. Come on, you two. Hurry up.
Flash	Here's a watch. I'll have that. I'll put it in the sack.
Billy	I'm going to take this cake and these chocolates. I'll give them to my old Dad.
Boss	Stop messing about, Billy. Grab some

	good stuff. We don't want cake and chocolates.
Flash	Here's a video-recorder, Boss.
Boss	Good! Get it in the sack!
Billy	Here's a nice torch, Boss. I'll put it in the sack.
Flash	Get off that torch, Billy. It's mine. I brought it with me.
Boss	What a fool. He's nicking our own stuff now. When I get this pot off my head I'm going to hit him with it!
Billy	Here's a little television, Boss. I've found a new camera, too.
Boss	That's better. Get them in the sack.
Flash	I think that's the lot, Boss.
Boss	Good! Let's get going. My head is killing me. It's not much fun inside this pot. Give me the sack and let's get away.
Flash	OK, let's go. Come here, Billy, let's get zipped up.
Billy	Here we go again. I hate being the back end of a reindeer.
Flash	I'll open the front door. Which way do we go, Boss?

Boss	How do I know? All I can see is the inside of this big white pot!
Flash	Let's go this way.
Billy	I hope we don't get lost in the fog. We might meet a copper.
Flash	Shh! Stop! Listen! I can hear somebody behind me!
Billy	It's me. It's Billy. I'm behind you in this reindeer outfit.
Flash	It's not you, you fool. I can hear somebody coming up behind us.
Snowman	Hello, hello, hello! What are you lot doing?
Boss	Who is it, Flash?
Flash	It's a snowman, Boss.
Boss	A snowman!? But it's not snowing, it's foggy.
Billy	He must be a fog-man, then.
Snowman	Who's that in the red coat with a lid on his head?
Flash	It's Santa Claus.
Snowman	It can't be Santa Claus. Santa Claus hasn't got a lid on his head. He's got a big white beard!

Billy	It's not a lid. It's a pot.
Snowman	Oh! Santa's gone potty!
Boss	What's that? Did you say that I'm potty? I'll smack you on the nose for that! Where are you!?

[*SMACK!!!*]

Flash	Ouch!! What did you hit me for?
Boss	Sorry, Flash. I was trying to hit the snowman. I can't see with this pot on my head.
Snowman	Pardon me for asking, but why have you got a pot on your head?
Boss	I stuck my head in to have a look around. Now I can't find my way out!
Flash	Who are you, anyway? Why are you dressed as a snowman?
Snowman	I'm a copper. I'm PC 48.
Boss	Gulp!
Billy	Gasp!
Flash	Merry Christmas!
Snowman	I'm on my way to the old people's home. It's their Christmas party. I'm going to give them some presents.

Flash	That's nice.
Snowman	And what are you lot doing?
Boss	Emmm ... we are helping people at Christmas too.
Billy	Yes, we are helping ourselves.
Flash	We've got presents in this sack.
Snowman	I hope they are for the old people!
Boss	Emmm ... yes, that's right. We are going to take these presents to some old people.
Snowman	Good, you're in luck. I'm going to see the old people now. I'll take your presents along with me. I'll save you the trip.
Boss	That's very nice of you, PC 48. I'll just ask my reindeer if that is OK. Flash, where are you?
Flash	I'm here, Boss. What are we going to do?
Boss	We'll have to give him the stuff. We'll be in trouble if we don't.
Flash	Oh no! All of this for nothing!
Boss	Here you are, PC 48. Here is the sack. You can give these presents to the old people from us.

Snowman	Thank you! Merry Christmas!
Boss	Now, can you tell us how to get to Nutt Street. That's where I live. We got lost in the fog.
Snowman	You won't have far to go. This is Nutt Street.
Boss	My goodness! I didn't know that I was so close to home!
Snowman	Well, I'll be seeing you.
Flash	Not if we see you first.
Snowman	Goodnight, thanks for the presents.
Boss	Has he gone?
Flash	Yes, Boss.
Boss	What a mess! We did all that work for nothing!
Flash	At least he didn't nick us. Come on, Boss. Let's find your house, then we can have a cup of tea.
Boss	And get this big white pot off my head!
Billy	Hello! Hello! Are you still there? Can you hear me?
Flash	Yes, Billy. Don't panic, we'll get you out of the reindeer outfit soon. What number is your house, Boss?

Boss	It's number 13.
Flash	Here it is. That's funny, the door is open. Watch your step!
Boss	Watch my what? Aaaagh!!

[*CRASH!!!!*]

Billy	What is it? Has Boss gone through the roof of the shed again?
Flash	No, Billy, he fell over the door-step and landed on his head. I mean he landed on his pot!
Boss	Oh, my head! What happened? Put the lights on!
Flash	You fell, Boss, and you smashed the pot!
Boss	Oh, yes, I can see. I'm in my own house.
Flash	Help us to get out of this reindeer outfit.
Boss	Come here and I'll pull the zip.
Billy	That's better. I can stand up again.
Boss	I'm going to make a nice cup of tea.
Flash	That's a good idea.
Boss	Oh no! Look at this!
Billy	What's the matter, Boss?

Boss	Look at my Christmas turkey! Somebody has been eating it! There's a big bite out of its leg!
Flash	There's a big bite out of its leg?
Billy	That's terrible!
Boss	And look at my Christmas tree. Somebody has been messing about with it!
Billy	Wait till I get my hands on him!
Boss	Oh, no! Look! Somebody has nicked my watch and my new camera!
Flash	Your watch and your new camera!?
Boss	They've nicked my video and my little television as well!
Flash	Your video and your television!?
Boss	Yes! My watch and my camera! My video and my television!
Billy	That's funny. That's what we have just nicked.
Flash	Just a minute! You've got an old shed at the back of your house, Boss!
Boss	That's right.
Flash	And look! The window at the top of your stairs is open!

Boss	Yes, and look, there's my best white flower-pot. My Ma gave it to me. It's all smashed up!
Flash	Do you know what we've done!?
Billy	Have we won the football pools?
Boss	No, you fool, we've robbed my house! Then we gave it all away!
Billy	Do you mean that we've been burgled?
Flash	No, Billy, we've been BUNGLED!!

Stories in the spirals series

Anita Jackson
The Actor
The Ear
The Austin Seven
Dreams
Bennet Manor
Pentag
No Rent to Pay
Doctor Maxwell
A Game of Life or Death

Jim Alderston
The Witch Princess
Crash in the Jungle

Jan Carew
Death Comes to the Circus

Susan Duberley
The Ring

**Keith Fletcher and
Susan Duberley**
Nightmare Lake

Paul Groves
The Third Climber

Paul Jennings
Eye of Evil
Maggot

Kevin Philbin
Summer of the Werewolf

John Townsend
Fame and Fortune
Beware the Morris Minor

Plays

Jan Carew
Time Loop
    Two short plays for seven to eight parts
No Entry
    Two short plays for seven to eight parts
Computer Killer
    Two short plays for six to seven parts

John Godfrey
When I Count to Three
    Three short plays for five to six parts

Nigel Gray
An Earwig in the Ear
    Three short plays for two parts

Paul Groves
Tell Me Where it Hurts
    Three short plays for two to five parts

Barbara Mitchelhill
Punchlines
    Six short plays for two to four parts
The Ramsbottoms at Home
    Three plays for four and five parts

Madeline Sotheby
Hard Times at Batwing Hall
    Two short plays for four to five parts

John Townsend
The End of the Line
    One play for a larger group
Taking the Plunge
    Three short plays for up to four parts
Cheer and Groan
    Two short plays for four parts
Hanging by a Fred
    One play for a larger group
Making a Splash
    Three short plays for two to four parts
Murder at Muckleby Manor
    One play for a larger group
Over and Out
    Two short plays for two parts

David Walke
The Good, the Bad and the Bungle
    Three short plays for three parts
Package Holiday
    Three short plays for four parts
The Bungle Gang Strikes Again
    Three short plays for four to six parts